COUNTRY PROFILE: COLOMBIA

COUNTRY

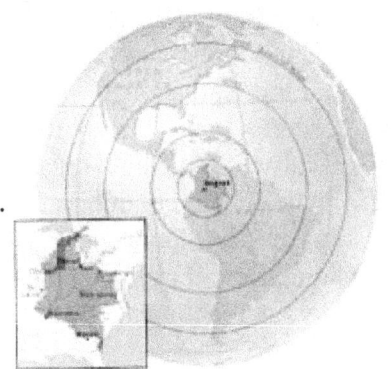

Click to Enlarge Image

Formal Name: Republic of Colombia (República de Colombia).

Short Form: Colombia.

Term for Citizen(s): Colombian(s).

Capital: Bogotá.

Major Cities: According to the 2005 census, the four cities with more than 1 million population are: Bogotá (4,300,000; Greater Bogotá, 6,776, 009), Medellín (2,223,078), Cali (2,068,386), and Barranquilla (1,380,437). These cities are also the four major industrial centers.

Independence: Colombia officially marks its independence from Spain on July 20, 1810, the date that criollo revolutionists established a ruling junta in the capital city of Santafé de Bogotá.

Public Holidays: Año Nuevo (New Year's Day) (January 1), Día de los Reyes Magos (Epiphany) (January 6*), Día de San José (St. Joseph's Day) (March 19*), Jueves Santo (Holy Thursday) and Viernes Santo (Holy Friday) (variable dates in March or April; in 2007: April 5 and April 6, respectively), Primero de Mayo (Labor Day) (May 1), Ascension Day (variable date; in 2007: May 17*), Corpus Christi (variable date; in 2007: June 7*), Sagrado Corazón (Sacred Heart) (June 18*), San Pedro y San Pablo (Saint Peter and Saint Paul) (June 29*), Independence Day (July 20), Battle of Boyacá (August 7), La Asunción (Assumption) (August 15*), Día de la Raza or Día de Colón (Columbus Day) (October 12*), Día de Todos los Santos (All Saints' Day) (November 1*), Independence of Cartagena City (November 11*), La Inmaculada Concepción (Immaculate Conception) (December 8), and Navidad (Christmas Day) (December 25). Note: * Movable holiday: when they do not fall on a Monday, these holidays are observed the following Monday.

Flag: Three horizontal bands of yellow (top, double-width), blue, and red.

Click to Enlarge Image

HISTORICAL BACKGROUND

Early History and Colonial Era: Colombia's pre-Columbian history began more than 20,000 years ago, according to the earliest evidence of human occupation. The Chibcha, sub-Andean (Arawak), and Caribbean (Carib) peoples, most of whom lived in a patchwork of separate but organized, agriculturally based communities, inhabited the area now called Colombia. By the early colonial period in the 1500s, the Chibcha had become the most advanced of the indigenous peoples.

In 1499 a Spanish expedition first visited the Guajira Peninsula of what is now Colombia. Following the Caribbean coast southwest, colonists founded the first important mainland settlement, Santa María la Antigua de Darién (what is now Acandí), on the Gulf of Urabá in 1510. The Spanish founded Santa Fe de Bogotá (present-day Bogotá) far inland—located on an eastern high plateau in the center of the country at an elevation of approximately 2,650 meters and bordered to the east by the Eastern Cordillera—in 1538, and it became the capital of the Viceroyalty of the New Kingdom of Granada in 1719. The Viceroyalty included present-day Venezuela, Ecuador, and Panama. The outbreak of war in Europe pushed Spain to increase taxation of the colonists in 1778 in order to fund the war. In 1781 anger over taxation led to New Granada's Revolt of the Comuneros (citizens organized to defend their rights against the arbitrary encroachment of government), an historic uprising that foreshadowed the revolution.

Independence: On July 20, 1810, revolutionary leaders took part in an uprising in Santa Fe de Bogotá that deposed the Spanish viceroy and created a governing council made up of criollos (persons of Spanish descent born in the New World). With the formation of their own governing body, the people of the region began favoring a complete break with Spain. On August 7, 1819, General Simón Bolívar (president, 1819–30) defeated the Spanish at the Battle of Boyacá, allowing the colonists to sever ties with Spain and form the Republic of Great Colombia (Gran Colombia), which included all territories under the jurisdiction of the Viceroyalty of New Granada (present-day Colombia, Panama, and Venezuela). Bolívar headed the government of Gran Colombia as president, with fellow liberator General Francisco de Paula Santander as his vice president. Although Gran Colombia became even greater in 1822, when Ecuador joined, the union would be short-lived. The followers of both leaders soon divided over conflicting political goals, setting the stage for the country's long history of political violence. Bolívar's supporters favored an authoritarian and centralized government, an alliance with the Roman Catholic Church, continuing slavery (despite his personal opposition to slavery), and a limited franchise. In contrast, the followers of Santander came to advocate a decentralized and federalist government, anticlericalism, and eventually broadened suffrage. When Ecuador and Venezuela seceded in 1830, Gran Colombia dissolved; what was left emerged as the Republic of New Granada, with Santander as its first president (1832–37).

After their official establishment in about 1850, the Conservative Party (Partido Conservador Colombiano—PCC) and the Liberal Party (Partido Liberal—PL) solidified the early ideological split between the Conservatives and Liberals. These two traditional political parties dominated Colombian politics for the next 150 years. From 1849 until 1886, Colombia oscillated between a liberal republic and a highly centralized, authoritarian government under several different constitutions and three different names. During two periods of Liberal dominance (1849–54 and 1861–80), the governments sought to reduce the power of the Roman Catholic Church, but those efforts were met with insurrection.

The Republic of Colombia: The 1886 constitution gave the country yet another name, the Republic of Colombia, reversed the federalist trend, and inaugurated 45 years of Conservative Party rule, during which time power was again centralized and church influence restored. Factionalism within the two main political parties and political and economic instability characterized the inaptly named Regeneration period from 1878 to 1900. These events led to the War of a Thousand Days (La Guerra de los Mil Días, 1899–1902) between the Liberals and the

Conservatives, a war that devastated the country and cost at least 100,000 lives. Panama seceded from the Republic of Colombia and, on November 3, 1903, declared independence.

In 1946 fighting again broke out following a change of parties in power, and in April 1948 the assassination of the popular Liberal leader Jorge Eliécer Gaitán led to a major outburst of rioting in Bogotá itself. The countrywide violence known as "La Violencia," in which as many as 300,000 people were killed, raged for more than 10 years. In 1958 the Conservatives and Liberals banded together to form the National Front, which helped to greatly reduce the violence in the early 1960s. Although the National Front arrangement ended in 1974, the tradition of presidents inviting opposition figures to hold cabinet positions continued through the 1990s.

The Era of Insurgency, Counterinsurgency, and Narcotrafficking: By excluding dissident political forces, the National Front pact contributed to the emergence of guerrilla groups in the mid-1960s. In 1965 the pro-Cuban National Liberation Army (Ejército de Liberación Nacional—ELN) and the Maoist People's Liberation Army (Ejército de Liberación Popular—EPL) were founded; the next year, the pro-Soviet Revolutionary Armed Forces of Colombia (Fuerzas Armadas Revolucionarias de Colombia—FARC) was founded and quickly became the largest guerrilla group. They were joined in 1974 by another left-wing insurgent group, the Nineteenth of April Movement (Movimiento 19 de April—M–19). Although the M–19 and EPL later demobilized and formed political parties (the former in 1989 and the latter in 1991), the ELN and FARC, as well as a dissident element of the EPL, have continued insurgent activities to the present day.

As Colombia became a world leader in the production and trafficking of illegal drugs in the 1970s and 1980s, the large drug syndicates such as the Medellín and Cali cartels gained wide power through terror and corruption. During the narco-terrorist era (1983–93), narcotics traffickers sponsored assassinations of numerous government officials, justices, and politicians, particularly those who favored an extradition treaty with the United States. The government broke up the Medellín Cartel in 1993 and later the Cali Cartel by arresting key leaders. Despite the setbacks, drug traffickers continued to fuel the civil conflict during the 1990s, as the illegal armed groups became increasingly dependent on the drug trade for financing their insurgent operations. Colombia's present constitution, adopted on July 5, 1991, replacing the 1886 charter, initially prohibited the extradition of Colombians wanted for trial in other countries. But drug traffickers have again faced extradition to the United States since 1997, when Colombia's Congress reinstated, by constitutional amendment, the extradition of Colombian nationals. Although the last of the big cartels, Norte del Valle, disintegrated in 2004, they have been replaced by hundreds of smaller, lower-profile cartels, many of which operate in association with the paramilitary and guerrilla groups. These smaller networks have continued to wield significant power, although they adopted discreet bribery and intimidation rather than the political assassinations that had resulted in government crackdowns and dismantlement of the larger drug cartels.

Strengthened by income from the illegal drug trade during the 1990s, the ELN and FARC extended their territorial presence in Colombia in 1996–98. The administration of Andrés Pastrana Arango (president, 1998–2002) was marked by high unemployment, increased countrywide attacks by the guerrilla groups, widespread drug production, and expansion of paramilitary groups. As a concession in exchange for beginning peace talks, Pastrana granted the FARC a 51,000-square-kilometer demilitarized zone (DMZ) in south-central Colombia in November 1998. However, the FARC used the DMZ as a haven to increase illicit drug crops, transport military equipment and provisions, and negotiate kidnappings and extortions. Since the collapse of this arrangement along with the peace talks in early 2002, both the FARC and ELN have continued their insurgencies.

Stepped-up government actions against the guerrillas during the first administration of Álvaro Uribe Vélez (president, 2002–6, 2006–), with the help of significant U.S. military aid, kept the guerrillas mostly withdrawn into the countryside, while government efforts to improve the economy and reduce cocaine production were showing results. Accordingly, the FARC devoted its efforts to making windfall profits from the trade in illegal drugs and maintaining its territorial control in its traditional, mostly rural areas of operation, which constitute at least 30 percent of the national territory. The FARC has used its huge revenue from drug trafficking to purchase a formidable guerrilla arsenal.

Paramilitary Partial Demobilization: The paramilitary groups that emerged in the early 1990s, including the United Self-Defense Forces of Colombia (Autodefensas Unidas de Colombia— AUC), the country's largest paramilitary organization, have fought the guerrilla groups and terrorized campesinos and human rights workers suspected of supporting or sympathizing with them. Members of these paramilitary groups are sometimes in the pay of drug cartels and landowners and backed by elements in the army and the police. After being formed in 1997, the AUC began operating as a loose confederation of disparate paramilitary groups, the largest of which is the Self-Defense Campesino Forces of Córdoba and Urabá (Autodefensas Campesinas de Córdoba y Urabá—ACCU). Other important paramilitary organizations include the Cacique Nutibara Bloc (Bloque Cacique Nutibara—BCN), the Central Bolívar Bloc (Bloque Central Bolívar—BCB), and the Middle Magdalena Bloc (Bloque del Magdalena Medio—BMM).

In July 2003, seven months after the AUC announced a unilateral cease-fire, the Uribe administration opened formal negotiations with the AUC with the goal of demobilizing it. On April 18, 2006, the government announced that the dismantlement process had been completed, with the formal demobilization, since 2003, of 30,150 paramilitaries, who surrendered about 17,000 weapons, 117 vehicles, three helicopters, 59 urban properties, and 24,000 hectares of land as part of the process mandated by the controversial Law of Justice and Peace of July 22, 2005. The Uribe government accepted most of the AUC's demands, which included minimal or complete absence of prison time to be served; no requirement to provide details of economic, political, or drug-trafficking structures; and a shield, but not total immunity, against extradition. Moreover, in addition to allowing the demobilized paramilitaries to retain substantial financial assets, the government gave political status to the AUC. An Organization of American States observer has monitored the government's peace process with the paramilitaries, lending the negotiations much-needed international credibility, although critics have complained about the leniency of the terms of surrender.

GEOGRAPHY

Click to Enlarge Image

Location: Colombia lies in the northwestern part of South America, bordered by the Caribbean Sea to the north and the North Pacific Ocean to the west.

Size: The fourth-largest country in South America, Colombia measures 1,138,910 square kilometers, including insular possessions and bodies of water, or slightly less than twice the size of Texas. Of this total, land constitutes 1,038,700 square kilometers and water, 100,210 square kilometers. The sizes of Colombia's islands in square kilometers are: Isla de Malpelo, 0.14; San Andrés y Providencia, 43 (Providencia Island, 17; San Andrés Island, 26); Roncador Cay, 65; Serrana Bank, 500; and Serranilla Bank, which is most mostly lagoons, 1,200.

Land Boundaries: Colombia's continental neighbors are Ecuador and Peru to the south, Brazil and Venezuela to the east, and the Isthmus of Panama to the west. Borders with neighboring countries total 6,004 kilometers, as follows: Ecuador, 590 kilometers; Peru, 1,496 kilometers (estimated); Brazil, 1,643 kilometers; Venezuela, 2,050 kilometers; and Panama, 225 kilometers.

Disputed Territory: Unresolved territorial disputes persist with Nicaragua and Venezuela. The issue of Nicaragua's alleged sovereignty rights over the Colombian islands of San Andrés y Providencia lying off the Caribbean coast of Nicaragua occasionally produces diplomatic disputes. Nicaragua revived the issue in 2002 by asking the International Court of Justice at The Hague to validate its claim. Colombia's dispute with Venezuela over substantial maritime territory lying off the Guajira Peninsula and in the Golfo de Venezuela (Gulf of Venezuela), an area popularly referred to by Colombians as the Golfo de Coquibacoa, is being resolved through bilateral negotiations, although elements of national prestige continue to make it a national issue in both countries.

Length of Coastline: The only South American country bordering both the Caribbean Sea and the Pacific Ocean, Colombia has a total of 3,208 kilometers of coastline—1,448 kilometers on the Pacific Ocean to the west and 1,760 kilometers on the Caribbean Sea to the north.

Maritime Claims: Colombia claims a 200-nautical mile exclusive economic zone, a 12-nautical mile territorial sea, and jurisdiction over the continental shelf to a 200-meter depth or to the depth of resource exploitation.

Topography: The mainland territory is divided into four major geographic regions. First, the coastal region consists of the Caribbean Lowlands and the Pacific Lowlands. Swamps separate the Caribbean Lowlands from the base of the Isthmus of Panama. The second region, encompassing the Central and Andean Highlands, consists of three rugged parallel mountain ranges (the Eastern Cordillera, the Central Cordillera, and the Western Cordillera), which constitute 33 percent of the country's land area. An isolated range, the Sierra Nevada de Santa Marta, rises on the Caribbean coast and includes Colombia's highest point at Pico Cristóbal

Colón (5,776 meters). The third region consists of the intervening high plateaus and fertile valley lowlands that are traversed mainly by three rivers: the Atrato, Sinú, and Magdalena. About 95 percent of the population resides in the narrow valleys and basins within the mountainous western part of the country. Finally, eastern Colombia includes the great plains (llanos) in the northern part and the tropical rainforest (*selva*) in the southern half. The llanos plain drains northeast into the Orinoco, while the *selva* drains southeast into the Amazon River Basin. Although eastern Colombia makes up about 54 percent of Colombia's territory, less than 3 percent of the total population resides in the nine eastern lowlands departments.

Principal Rivers: Colombia has 20,000 kilometers of rivers. Its principal rivers are the Magdalena, 1,540 kilometers; the Putumayo, 1,500 kilometers; and the Cauca, 1,014 kilometers. The Cauca and Magdalena, which flow northward, divide the three principal Andean mountain ranges and join after emerging from the mountains and descending through marshy lowlands to the Caribbean near Barranquilla. In the west, the Patía flows through the Andes and empties into the Pacific. A total of 18,140 kilometers of waterways are navigable by riverboats.

Climate: Mainly as a result of differences in elevation, Colombia has a striking variety in temperatures, with little seasonal variation. The habitable areas of the country are divided into three climatic zones: hot (*tierra caliente*; below 900 meters in elevation), temperate (*tierra temblada*; 900–2,000 meters), and cold (*tierra fría*; 2,000 meters to about 3,500 meters). The hottest month is March, and the coldest months are July and August. Precipitation is generally moderate to heavy, with the highest levels in the Pacific Lowlands and in parts of eastern Colombia. Considerable year-to-year variations are recorded, but generally most of the country has two main wet seasons with heavy daily rainfall (March to May and September to November) and one or two dry seasons with little or no rainfall (December to February and June to August), except in the northern plains, where there is only one long wet season from May through October. The wettest month is October, and the driest month is February. Average annual precipitation is 3,000 millimeters. Average temperature ranges in Bogotá, which has an elevation of 2,560 meters, vary little, for example, 10° C–18° C in July and 9° C–20° C in February.

Natural Resources: Colombia is well endowed with agricultural export products, energy resources, and minerals. These resources include coal, coffee, copper, emeralds, flowers, fruits, gas, gold, hydropower, iron ore, natural nickel (also known as Millerite, a compound that is a natural nickel sulphide), petroleum, platinum, and silver. Colombia ranks first in Latin America for its coal reserves (with 7.4 billion metric tons of proven and recoverable reserves), fourth for natural gas (proven commercial reserves of around 114.4 billion cubic meters as of 2005, or enough to last until about 2022); and sixth for oil (1.4 billion proven barrels at the end of 2005, or enough to prevent Colombia from becoming a net oil importer until 2010–11). In addition, the country is second only to Brazil in hydroelectric potential. Potential natural gas reserves in offshore basins along the Caribbean Coast are estimated to cover 150 to 200 years of consumption. Most of the natural gas reserves are located in the Llanos Basin in the foothills of the Eastern Cordillera.

Land Use: Colombia's arable land is located mostly in patches on the Andean mountainsides. In 2005 an estimated 2.01 percent of the total land area was arable (approximately 21,000–23,000 square kilometers). The amount of arable land apparently has declined since 2003, when it was estimated to be 28,880 square kilometers. An estimated 1.37 percent of the total land area (14,230 square kilometers) was planted to permanent crops in 2005. Irrigated land totaled 9,000 square kilometers in 2003.

Environmental Factors: The 1991 constitution codifies new environmental protection legislation, including the creation of specially protected zones, of which Colombia had 443 in 2003, mostly in forest areas and national parks. Colombia has an extraordinarily high percentage of its total land area designated as a protected area (72.3 percent in 2003). Current environmental issues include deforestation resulting from lumber exploitation in the jungles of the Amazon and the region of Chocó on the Pacific coast. In 2004 about half of Colombia's territory, or 607,300 square kilometers (2,300 square kilometers less than in 2000), was forested area. Other issues include illicit drug crops grown by campesinos in the national parks of Sierra de la Macarena and Sierra Nevada de Santa Marta, soil erosion, soil and water quality damage from contamination by the use of chemicals in the coca-refining process, spillage of crude oil into the local rivers caused by guerrilla sabotage of pipelines and overuse of pesticides (and herbicides to eradicate the coca crop), air pollution (especially in Bogotá) from vehicle emissions, and endangerment of wildlife. The government's use of herbicides has compounded the environmental degradation. As a result of soil erosion, 65 percent of the country's municipalities are facing water shortages by 2015. Although 93 percent of the population had access to improved water sources and 86 percent to adequate sanitation facilities in 2004, only about one-third of Colombia's 1,098 municipalities have adequate treatment systems for contaminated waters.

Time Zone: Colombia Standard Time is five hours behind Greenwich Mean Time (GMT–5).

SOCIETY

Population: Colombia is the third most populous country in Latin America, after Brazil and Mexico. According to the official final number compiled by the 2005 national census conducted by the National Administrative Department of Statistics (Departamento Administrativo Nacional de Estadística—DANE), the national population was 41,468,384 in 2005. This adjusted figure takes into account geographical coverage omissions but does not include Colombians living abroad. According to the 2005 census, the population growth rate during 2001–5 was 1.6 percent. The estimated population growth rate in 2006 was 1.46 percent.

Colombia has a largely urban population. By 2005 the urban population had increased to 75 percent from 57 percent of the total population in 1951, according to the DANE census. About 35 percent of the total population is concentrated in four cities: Bogotá, Medellín, Cali, and Barranquilla. Estimates of population density (inhabitants per square kilometer) have varied, ranging from 37 in 2000 to 44 in 2005. Moreover, population distribution throughout the country is very skewed. Population density in the eastern departments is less than one person per square kilometer.

The net migration rate in 2006 was –0.3 migrant(s) per 1,000 population. Migration from rural to urban areas has been prevalent. The move to urban areas reflects not only a shift away from agriculture but also a flight from guerrilla and paramilitary violence. According to the 2005 census, 1,542,915 Colombians were victims of forced displacement between 1995 and 2005, but the actual number may be between 2 and 3 million, according to nongovernmental organizations (NGOs). More than 3.5 million Colombians have been displaced since 1985, according to the Consultancy for Human Rights and Displacement (La Consultoría para los Derechos Humanos y el Desplazamiento—Codhes), an authoritative NGO source. Almost 1 million people have been displaced since the government of President Álvaro Uribe Vélez took office in 2002, according to Codhes and official sources. Codhes recorded more than 250,000 newly displaced people in 2005, or 90,000 more than the government's figure.

Owing to problems of security and unemployment, a total of 1.2 million Colombians abandoned the country legally during 2000–5 and have not returned. According to the 2005 census, 3,331,107 Colombians were living abroad. According to other estimates, the actual figure may exceed 4 million, or almost 10 percent of the country's population. External migration is primarily to Ecuador, the United States, and Venezuela.

Demography: Colombia has a relatively young population, with a large percentage in the 0–14 age-group and about 80 percent of the population under age 45. The median age in 2006 was estimated at 26.3 years (25.4 years for males and 27.2 years for females). The estimated age profile of the population in 2006 was 30.3 percent in the 0–14 age-group, 64.5 percent in the 15–64 age-group, and 5.2 percent in the 65 and older age-group. According to the 2005 census, 48.8 percent of the population was male and 51.2 percent female. According to 2006 estimates, the birthrate was 20.48 per 1,000 population; the infant mortality rate was 20.35 deaths per 1,000 live births; life expectancy at birth for the total population was 71.99 years (males, 68.15 years; females, 75.96 years); the estimated total fertility rate was 2.54 children born per woman; and the estimated death rate was 5.58 deaths per 1,000 population. In 2004 the under-five mortality rate per 1,000 population was 24 for males and 17 for females, and the adult mortality rate per 1,000 population between 15 and 60 years of age was 226 for males and 93 for females. The greater number of male homicide victims accounts for the significant gap between life expectancy and the probability of dying for men and women.

The 2005 census found that approximately 66.7 percent of Colombian homes had four or fewer persons, and the average number was 3.9. It also determined that 44.9 percent of Colombians were single, 23 percent married, and 23.1 percent over 10 years of age were living together as unmarried couples.

Official Language: Spanish.

Ethnic Groups and Languages: The 2005 census defines ethnic groups as being the Afro-Colombian, indigenous, and gypsy populations. It defines the Afro-Colombian population as including blacks, mulattoes (mixed black and white ancestry), and *zambos* (mixed Indian and black ancestry). Although ethnic estimates vary widely, the census found that the Afro-Colombian population accounted for 10.5 percent of the national population; the indigenous population, for 3.4 percent; and the gypsy population, for 0.01 percent. The census also reported that the "nonethnic population" (whites and mestizos—those of mixed white and Amerindian ancestry) constituted 86 percent of the national population. Estimates of the mestizo category, to which almost all of the urban business and political elite belong, range from 54 percent to 58 percent of Colombia's national population. Estimates of the category of unmixed white ancestry range from 20 percent to 40 percent.

The upper class, constituting 5 percent of the population, is overwhelmingly white; the middle class, 20 percent, is mostly mestizo; and the lower class, 75 percent, is proportionately mestizo, Afro-Colombian, and indigenous. The populations of major cities are primarily white and mestizo. Most indigenous people and Afro-Colombians live in rural areas—the former in barren and inaccessible regions and the latter in the Caribbean and Pacific coastal regions and tropical valleys.

The country has as many as 98 languages, of which 78 are living and 20 extinct. There are about 500,000 speakers of Amerindian languages, which include Wayuu, Camsá, and Cuaiquer, but their numbers are diminishing rapidly.

Religion: Article 19 of the 1991 constitution, building on the Concordat of 1973, gives Colombians the right to freely practice their religion on an equal basis with Roman Catholicism, which was traditionally the country's official religion. The government generally respects this right in practice. However, for political reasons the illegal armed groups, both left-wing and paramilitary, have targeted religious leaders and practitioners, killing, kidnapping, or extorting them and thereby inhibiting free religious expression. An estimated 95 percent of Colombians (or only 87 percent, according to a low estimate) are at least nominally Roman Catholics, and the Roman Catholic Church enjoys a de facto privileged status. About 3 percent of Colombians are members of various Protestant groups. The remaining 2 percent, mostly Afro-Colombians, often engage in syncretic religious practices that blend forms of spirit worship with Roman Catholicism.

Education and Literacy: Total public spending on education constituted 4.8 percent of gross domestic product in 2004, one of the highest rates in Latin America. The ratio of pupils to teachers in 2001 was 26:1 in primary school and 19:2 in secondary school. The school year extends from February to November. Primary education for children between six and 12 years of age is free and compulsory for nine years, but in many rural areas teachers are poorly qualified, and only five years of primary school are offered. The net primary completion rate (percentage of relevant age-group) in 2004 was 94.3 percent. Secondary education (*educación media*) begins at age 11 and lasts up to six years, without any opportunity for vocational training. Secondary-school graduates are awarded the *bachillerato* (high-school diploma). Net secondary enrollment in 2004 was 74.5 percent. Tertiary school enrollment in 2004 as a percentage of gross was 26.9 percent. Colombia has 24 public universities.

According to the 2005 census, almost 11 million students attended primary and secondary schools. Of these students, 8,310,165 were in public schools and 2,475,304 in private schools. The census found that the percentages of the population enrolled in a formal educational establishment were 50.3 percent for those between three and five years of age, 90.7 percent for those between six and 10 years of age, and 79.9 percent for those between 11 and 17 years of age. The census data also indicated that 37.2 percent of the population had attained basic primary education; 31.7 percent, secondary; 7 percent, professional; and 1.3 percent, specialized studies (master's or doctorate). The percentage of the population without any education was 10.5

percent. According to the census, 88.3 percent of the total population five years of age or older could read and write. This percentage varies depending on the age-group used. For example, according to a 2004 estimate, a total of 92.8 percent of the population 15 years of age or older is literate. Although literacy for males and females in this age-group is almost 93 percent in urban areas, it is only 67 percent in rural areas.

Health: Health standards in Colombia have improved greatly since the 1980s. A 1993 reform transformed the structure of public health-care funding by shifting the burden of subsidy from providers to users. As a result, employees have been obligated to pay into health plans to which employers also contribute. Although this new system has widened population coverage by the social and health security system from 21 percent (pre-1993) to 56 percent in 2004 and 66 percent in 2005, health disparities persist, with the poor continuing to suffer relatively high mortality rates. In 2002 Colombia had 58,761 physicians, 23,950 nurses, and 33,951 dentists; these numbers equated to 1.35 physicians, 0.55 nurses, and 0.78 dentists per 1,000 population, respectively. In 2005 Colombia was reported to have only 1.1 physicians per 1,000 population, as compared with a Latin American average of 1.5. The health sector reportedly is plagued by rampant corruption, including misallocation of funds and evasion of health-fund contributions.

General government spending on health accounted for 20.5 percent of total government expenditures and for 84.1 percent of total health expenditures (private expenditures made up the balance) in 2003. Total expenditures on health constituted 5.6 percent of gross domestic product in 2005. The per capita expenditure on health care in 2005 at an average exchange rate was US$150.

Since 2001–2 Colombia has halved its homicide rate, which was more than 60 per 100,000 inhabitants, or 28,837, in 2002, one of the world's highest homicide rates. In 2006 a total of 17,206 violent deaths were recorded, the lowest figure since 1987. Other than homicide, heart disease is the main cause of premature death, followed by strokes, respiratory diseases, road accidents, and diabetes. Waterborne diseases such as cerebral malaria and leishmaniasis are prevalent in lowland and coastal areas. Child immunization for measles in 2004 as a percentage of children under 12 months of age was 92 percent.

Acquired immune deficiency syndrome (AIDS) is the fifth-leading cause of death in the working-age population. According to Colombia's National Health Institute data reported in 2003, nearly 240,000 people—mostly women and young people—or 0.6 percent of the population had been infected with the virus since AIDS arrived in Colombia in October 1983. Estimates of the number of people living with human immunodeficiency virus (HIV), adults and children (0–49 years of age), in 2005 ranged from 160,000 to 310,000. The comparable figure for women (15–49 years of age) was 62,000. The number of AIDS and hepatitis B cases has been rising. In 2005 the estimated HIV adult prevalence rate (15–49 years of age) was 0.6 percent. As of 2006, between 5,200 and 12,000 people had died from AIDS. Services provided by the new Multisectoral National Plan, launched in July 2004, include integrated care for people living with HIV and provision of antiretroviral drugs. Under the plan, about 12,000 people have been receiving combined antiretroviral therapy (approximately 54 percent of those requiring it).

Welfare: All Colombian workers are legally required to be affiliated with a basic pension and health provider. The Social Security Institute (Instituto de Seguros Sociales—ISS) is one of Colombia's largest state companies and is the principal agency involved in the social security field, with responsibility for health care, pensions, and professional risks. In the private sector, workers can choose between the private system based on individual accounts or the state-run system. Employers and employees contribute jointly to a unified social security system. In mid-2005, private pension funds had approximately 6.1 million account holders, and private pension funds had become the largest institutional investors in Colombia. Pension liabilities have been rising in Colombia as a result of corruption and the government's failure to pay into the system as originally planned or to readjust contributions. A pension reform approved in mid-2005 reduced annual pension payments from 14 percent to 13 percent and eliminated privileged pension benefits. The number of retirees in the ISS system starting in 2008 was expected to increase from 819,000 to 955,000. From 2009 on, the government will have to bear the increased cost of allowing women to retire at age 55 and men to retire at age 60, with 75 percent of the final basic wage if they had paid in 1,000 weeks or 90 percent if they had paid in 1,250 weeks by that date.

Serious social problems include high rates of criminal violence, extensive societal discrimination against women, child abuse, and child prostitution; trafficking in women and girls for the purpose of sexual exploitation; widespread child labor; extensive societal discrimination against indigenous people and minorities; drug addiction; poverty; and displacement of the rural population. The 2005 government census found that about 800,000 children between the ages of 12 and 17 work in Colombia. The only industry identified in Colombia that uses child labor and directly exports to the United States is the flower agribusiness, where children are used in both the processing and harvesting of flowers. The number of children (0–17 years of age) orphaned from all causes was 910,000 at the end of 2003.

After having reached a low of 50 percent in 1997, the proportion of the population living below the poverty line exceeded 60 percent in 2005, according to the Comptroller General's Office. However, the Colombian government's official estimate was just under 49.2 percent in 2005. The government estimated that the percentage of the population living in extreme poverty in 2005 was 15 percent, down from 26 percent in 2002, although in rural areas the incidence of extreme poverty could be as high as 40 percent.

ECONOMY

Overview: In 2006 Colombia had the fifth-largest economy in Latin America, a status that is expected to continue through 2010. Since the liberalization of the economy under the new constitution of 1991, the government has sought to facilitate the gradual transition from a highly regulated economy to a free-market economy through measures such as tariff reductions, financial deregulation, privatization of state-owned enterprises, and adoption of a more liberal foreign-exchange rate. Although the economy became mired in a recession in 1998–99 as a result of external shocks and monetary tightening to curb inflation, it has rebounded since 2003 as a result of confidence in the political and economic policies of President Álvaro Uribe Vélez. The recovery of growth in the gross domestic product (GDP) in 2005 and an overall reduction in criminal and political violence contributed to the favorable conditions that enabled President Uribe to be reelected in May 2006 with a strengthened popular mandate. The economy is expected to remain steady despite continuing weak domestic and foreign demand, slow GDP growth, austere government budgets, and serious internal armed conflict.

Gross Domestic Product (GDP): Overall GDP increased in real terms by an average of 2.5 percent a year from 1990 to 2002. The real GDP growth indicated that the economy—driven by exports, private investment, and a recovery of household consumption—had rebounded from a GDP growth rate of –4.2 percent in 1999. The upward trend has continued, reaching an estimated 6.1 percent in 2006, although this growth was expected to slow to 4.9 percent in 2007. The GDP totaled an estimated US$133.7 billion in 2006. The estimated origins of GDP by sector in 2006 were agriculture, 12 percent; industry, 35.2 percent (including manufacturing, about 15 percent); and services, 52.7 percent.

Colombia is a lower middle-income country. Real GDP per capita contracted by 6 percent in 1998–2002 and only recovered its 1997 level in 2005, when it reached US$2,290 (or US$7,661 at purchasing power parity). In 2005 the median household income was US$3,904. The estimated GDP per capita for 2006 was US$2,823, a figure that was expected to decline to US$2,791 in 2007 at market exchange rates.

Government Budget: Favorable international conditions such as higher oil prices and Colombia's economic expansion aided the efforts of the Uribe administration to bring Colombia's public finances under control. In 2005 the government had revenues estimated at US$46.8 billion and expenditures estimated at US$48.8 billion. The estimated 2006 budget deficit was 5.1 percent of gross domestic product (GDP), as compared with 5 percent of GDP in 2005. The growing public-sector debt was about 46 percent of GDP in 2006. Under President Uribe's approved second-term reforms of the tax regime, the income tax rate will decline gradually to 35 percent in 2007, 34 percent in 2008, and 33 percent in 2009, while corporate taxes will be lowered and the value-added tax (VAT) simplified.

Inflation: During 1990–2002, the inflation rate averaged 18.1 percent per year, but it gradually fell to an estimated 4.3 percent in 2006. It was expected to remain about the same in 2007–8.

Agriculture, Forestry, and Fishing: Since 2003 the Colombian Institute of Rural Development has managed the agricultural and fishing industries. Agriculture's share of gross domestic product (GDP) has declined significantly since 1987, when it was almost 21 percent of GDP. During 1990–2001, its share of GDP decreased at an average annual rate of 1.1 percent. In 2006 agriculture accounted for an estimated 12 percent of GDP and employed 22.7 percent of the labor force. Approximately 15 percent of Colombia's total exports come from agriculture, including livestock and fishing.

A diverse climate and topography allow cultivation of a wide variety of crops. Products include bananas, beef, cassava, cocoa, coffee, corn, cotton, cut flowers, livestock, palm oil, potatoes, rice, soybeans, sugarcane, timber, and tobacco. Coffee remains Colombia's leading legal cash and export crop, accounting for 6.9 percent of export earnings in 2005 (about US$1.6 billion) and about one-third of employment in agriculture (600,000 people). However, Colombia's arable land has been used increasingly to cultivate coca for cocaine production. Moreover, endemic guerrilla and paramilitary violence has been a serious problem for many campesinos and cattle ranch owners, and it has discouraged investment in the sector. Consequently, sectoral growth has been declining, from 4 percent in 2004 to 2 percent in 2005.

Colombia has from 53 to 58 million hectares of forest and woodland, only 3 million hectares of which are dedicated to commercial exploitation. The Institute of Hydrology and Environmental Studies estimated in 2004 that Colombia lost around 101,000 hectares of forest in the period from 1994 to 2001. The government is offering incentives to increase forest and woodland by 1.5 million hectares between 2002 and 2025. Roundwood removals in 2004 totaled 8.1 million cubic meters, and sawnwood production totaled 622,000 cubic meters. Much of the harvested wood is used as fuel.

The fisheries and aquaculture sector, which employed 88,000 people in 2001, accounts for less than a quarter of the agriculture sector's percentage of national production. Low fish consumption and rudimentary fishing techniques apparently account for the relatively marginal performance of the fishing industry, despite a huge potential for both aquaculture and sea fishing along Colombia's 3,208 kilometers of coastline. The total catch in 2004 was 211,385 metric tons. Authorized and unauthorized foreign ships commonly fish in Colombian waters.

Mining and Minerals: Despite its immense hydrocarbon potential, only 20 percent of Colombia's potential reserves are currently in production. Total crude oil production averaged 526,000 barrels per day in 2005, down from 810,000 barrels per day in 1999. The steady decline is due to a lack of sizable new reserve discoveries. Declining domestic oil production means that Colombia will have to import oil in the medium to long term. With its limited refining capacity, the country is already importing some refined products, especially gasoline and fuel oils. The country's current refining capacity is about 300,000 barrels per day. Colombia is the world's tenth-largest producer of hard coal, with coal production in 2005 totaling 59 to 61 million metric tons. About 90 percent of domestic coal production, which is entirely handled by foreign companies, is exported. In 2005 Colombia was the world's sixth-largest coal exporter, ranking after China and ahead of the United States. It was also the largest producer in Latin America of ferronickel in 2005 (39,700 metric tons).

Natural gas production and consumption each totaled an estimated 6.18 billion cubic meters in 2004. Gas for the domestic market is produced at the Cusiana–Cupiagua oil and gas fields in the northeastern province of Casanare in the Llanos Basin. However, the Guajira Basin accounts for most current production. More than 60 percent of natural gas demand comes from the Atlantic coastal region in Guajira Department, where industry and the electricity sector are the main users.

Industry and Manufacturing: Industry accounted for 35.2 percent of gross domestic product (GDP) in 2006, including about 15 percent for manufacturing. Industry's share of employment in 2006 was 18.7 percent. Manufacturing has been expanding rapidly since May 2006. Major manufactured products include beverages, cardboard containers, cement, chemicals, electrical equipment, machinery, metal products, pharmaceuticals, plastic resins and manufactures, textiles and garments, transport equipment, and wood products. In late 2000, construction began recovering from a major five-year downturn and was the fastest-growing subsector, driving GDP growth in 2003–5; it jumped from a 9.1 percent GDP growth rate in 2004 to 27.6 percent in 2005. Construction contributed an estimated 6.7 percent of GDP in 2005.

Energy: Colombia is self-sufficient in energy. Electricity-generating capacity has remained at nearly 13.5 gigawatts since the mid-1990s. Of that total, an average of 66 percent was hydroelectric and 34 percent thermal. With installed electricity-generating capacity of 13.4 gigawatts in 2004, Colombia produced 46,571 gigawatt-hours of electricity; hydropower accounted for 78 percent of the electricity; thermal power, 21 percent; and other renewable sources, 1 percent. The country's heavy dependence on hydroelectric generation makes it vulnerable to disruptions caused by drought. As a result of Colombia's great potential in terms of its coal, gas, and oil reserves, the energy sector accounts for 51 percent of total investment.

Services: The services sector accounted for 52.7 percent of gross domestic product (GDP) in 2006. In the first trimester of 2006, the services sector's share of employment was 60 percent. This sector includes commerce; communications; electricity, gas, and water; financial services; tourism; and transportation.

Representing nearly 18 percent of GDP, financial services are centered in Bogotá, Medellín, and, to a lesser extent, Cali. The banking sector has been consolidating since 2004, when domestic banks reportedly controlled 84 percent of the assets and foreign banks, 16 percent. The foreign-owned banks generally cater to multinational corporations and high-income customers. The total number of domestic banks (commercial and mortgage) was reduced to 10 in 2006. The financial system is characterized by a multi-banking model, although only two banking groups own almost half the country's bank assets. The Bank of the Republic (Banco de la República—Banrep) operates as the central bank. Since the government bailed out the banking sector in 1999 at a cost of 7 percent of GDP, most banks have been modernizing and by mid-2001 had returned to profitability. Online banking transactions increased by 67 percent from 2004 to 2005. Since its creation in 2005, the Financial Superintendency, a new financial authority, has supervised and regulated the banking sector as well as public companies and private pension funds, in coordination with the Ministry of Finance and Public Credit and two other agencies. Since the Bogotá, Cali, and Medellín stock markets merged in 2002 to create the Colombian Securities Exchange (Bolsa de Valores de Colombia—BVC), the BVC has received massive inflows of domestic investment. From US$24.6 billion at the end of 2004, market capitalization soared to US$50.7 billion at the end of 2005.

Growth of tourism has been slow for several decades because of the country's reputation for criminal, political, and narcotics-related violence and remains a marginal activity, even though conditions have improved under the Uribe government. Colombia remains on the U.S. Department of State's list of 31 countries with "travel warnings." Although the tourism sector accounts for only about 1 percent of GDP, it is an important foreign-exchange earner. International tourism receipts totaled US$1.3 billion in 2005 and an estimated US$1.5 billion in 2006. Despite low rates of tourism, reduced violence in recent years has allowed hotel occupancy rates to begin to recover, reaching 63 percent in 2006. Relatively isolated and safe tourism areas on the Caribbean, such as Cartagena and Santa Marta and the Caribbean islands of San Andrés and Providencia, are among the most popular Colombian tourism destinations. However, Bogotá was the most popular Colombian city for international visitors in 2005. The government has been promoting road travel and providing incentives for hotel construction and tourist projects in natural parks and ecological sites such as the Amazon and the coffee zone. One of the most rapidly growing subsectors of Colombian tourism is ecotourism.

Labor: During 2001–5, the working-age population grew by 1.9 percent and the labor force by 1.4 percent. Colombia has a generally well-educated and trained workforce, which totaled an estimated 20.5 million people in 2005. Trade union militancy has declined in recent decades as a result of high unemployment, the loss of prestige of the unions, and paramilitary attacks on union members. The local business community is represented by the Union Council, which is a federation of sectoral interests. Although nonskilled labor wages are protected from declining in real terms by strict minimum-wage regulation, businesses have reduced skilled labor wages and increased layoffs.

The national unemployment rate has declined since 2000, when it reached a high of 19.7 percent. By 2005 it had dropped to an estimated 11.8 percent, but it rose to 12.7 percent in the third quarter of 2006, possibly because of a new accounting methodology. Despite the uptick, the gradual downward trend is expected to continue over the next 10 years as the working-age population expands more slowly than the population in general. Underemployment, which has affected more than 30 percent of the working population since 2001, also rose in the third quarter of 2006 to 35.4 percent, as compared with 32.6 percent in 2005.

Foreign Economic Relations: The United States has long been Colombia's most important trading partner. Colombia and the United States reached agreement on a major Andean free-trade agreement in February 2006, and the George W. Bush administration signed it on November 22, 2006. However, U.S. congressional reservations remained, and congressional ratification in both countries is needed in order for it to come into effect in 2008. Colombian exports to the Andean countries—including Venezuela, traditionally Colombia's second-largest trading partner—have accounted for about 20 percent of total Colombian exports since 2000. Colombia has signed free-trade agreements with Chile, Mexico, and Venezuela, as well as with the Caribbean Community and Common Market (Caricom). The Uribe administration strongly favors extending these bilateral trade agreements across the hemisphere. Another principal destination for Colombian exports is the European Union (EU). Germany is Colombia's principal EU trading partner. Both the United States and the EU grant preferential access to Colombian exports under the Generalized Preferences System.

Imports: Aided by currency appreciation, imports have soared since 1991, when the government cut tariffs and eliminated nontariff barriers on imports. Imports of goods (free on board—f.o.b.) amounted to an estimated US$22.8 billion in 2006. The trend of rising imports is expected to continue, totaling a projected US$27.7 billion in 2007. The major suppliers of imported goods in 2005 were the United States, 28.1 percent; Venezuela, 6.4 percent; Mexico, 5.9 percent; and Brazil, 5.5 percent. Colombia's principal imports include machinery, industrial and oil and gas industry equipment, grains, chemicals, transportation equipment, mineral products, consumer products, metal and metal products, plastic and rubber, paper products, and aircraft supplies.

Exports: Exports of goods (free on board—f.o.b) amounted to an estimated US$23.5 billion in 2006. The trend of increasing exports has reflected higher commodity prices and growing foreign demand, as well as the Uribe government's export-oriented strategy. Traditional exports—oil, coal, coffee, and nickel—reached US$5 billion in 2005. Although coffee represented 60 percent of exports in 1987, in 2005 it was in third place behind oil and coal because of low international prices in recent years. Colombia exports about half of its oil production, with most of it (156,000 barrels per day) going to the United States. Oil exports generate about US$2 billion a year and represent more than 20 percent of Colombia's exports and about 4.5 percent of the gross domestic product (GDP). Exports of coal rose to US$2.6 billion in 2005, or 12.3 percent of total exports. Despite relatively high prices, export volumes of coal fell by 16 percent and coffee by 6 percent in the first half of 2006. Although oil volumes increased only slightly during this period, revenues from Colombia's most valuable export increased by 35 percent because of higher international prices. The most significant nontraditional exports include agricultural products (cut flowers, bananas, and sugar), mining products (ferronickel, gold, cement, and emeralds), and industrial products (textiles and apparel, chemicals, pharmaceuticals, cardboard containers, printed material, plastic resins, and manufactures). The main destinations of exports in 2005 were the United States, 40.4 percent; Venezuela, 9.2 percent; Ecuador, 5.7 percent; and Peru, 3.5 percent.

Balance of Trade: Exports grew faster than imports during the 1999–2006 period, allowing Colombia to report positive trade balances. Exports of goods (free on board—f.o.b.) amounted to an estimated US$23.5 billion and imports of goods f.o.b. to an estimated US$22.8 billion in 2006.

Balance of Payments: The current account showed a deficit of an estimated US$2.2 billion in 2006, or about 1.7 percent of gross domestic product. The estimated current-account deficit during 2006–10 is expected to widen as a result of a rising import bill and higher debt interest payments. Although the current-account deficit has been growing in recent years, it was more than offset in 2005 by a high surplus of US$3.3 billion on the capital account. (The capital account totaled US$38.7 billion in 2005.) Moreover, the deficit has continued to be fully covered by long-term financing flows, including foreign direct investment and remittances. Colombia's foreign currency reserves (in convertible foreign currencies) totaled an estimated US$16.3 billion in 2006.

External Debt: Colombia's foreign debt remains one of the country's main weaknesses. The external debt rose to an estimated US$35.1 billion in 2006 and was projected to continue rising. The paid debt-service ratio as a percentage of annual export earnings was an estimated 28.2 percent in 2006.

Foreign Investment: Foreign direct investment (FDI) has grown strongly since the early 1990s, when the government passed laws to stimulate foreign investment in nearly all sectors of the economy by eliminating restrictions on foreign inflows, creating a privatization program, and opening foreign investment in the oil industry. The central bank reported that FDI jumped to US$10.1 billion in 2005 (from US$3.2 billion in 2004), mainly as a result of the acquisition of two of Colombia's largest corporations (beer and tobacco producers) by investors in South Africa and the United States. In 2005 the sectors with the largest FDI inflows were manufacturing (53 percent of the total of US$10.2 billion), mining and quarrying (19 percent), and oil (12 percent). In 2005 the United Kingdom, with 37 percent of total investments, was the main source of FDI, followed by the United States, with 14 percent. Areas closed to FDI include defense and national security, disposal of hazardous wastes, and real estate. The government also reserves ownership in strategic areas such as natural resources, but foreign companies may participate in exploration and exploitation.

Currency and Exchange Rate: Colombia's currency is the peso (pl., pesos), which equals 100 centavos. Peso banknotes are issued in the following denominations: 1,000, 2,000, 5,000, 10,000, 20,000, and 50,000 pesos. The peso is formally abbreviated as COP and informally as COL$ or Ps. After modest devaluations in 1999–2002, the peso appreciated in 2004–5 as a result of increased remittances from Colombians working abroad, foreign direct investment, and portfolio investment. It began depreciating in March 2006 and lost about 5 percent of its value during the next six months. The peso ended 2006 trading at Ps2,239 per US$1, similar to its level at the end of 2005. Its average exchange rate in 2006 was Ps2,404 per US$1. The average exchange rate forecast for 2007 is Ps2,570 per US$1. The peso is expected to continue depreciating to approximately Ps2,900 per US$1 at the end of 2010 because of the growing current-account deficit.

Fiscal Year: Calendar year.

TRANSPORTATION AND TELECOMMUNICATIONS

Overview: Road travel is the main means of transport; almost 70 percent of cargo is transported by road, as compared with 27 percent by railroad, 3 percent by internal waterways, and 1 percent by air. Nevertheless, Colombia has one of the lowest ratios of paved roads per inhabitant in Latin America. The country has well-developed air and waterway routes. The only means of transportation in 40 percent of the country is via waterways, but guerrilla groups control the waterways in the south and southeast.

Urban transport systems have been developed in Bogotá and Medellín. Traffic congestion in Bogotá has been greatly exacerbated by the lack of rail transport. However, this problem has been alleviated somewhat by the development of the TransMilenio Bus Rapid System and the restriction of vehicles through a daily, rotating ban on private cars depending on plate numbers. Bogotá's system consists of bus and minibus services managed by both private- and public-sector enterprises. Since 1996 Medellín has had a modern urban railway referred to as the Metro de Medellín, which also connects with the cities of Itagüí, Envigado, and Bello. An elevated cable car system, Metro Cable, was added in 2004 to link some of Medellín's poorer mountainous neighborhoods with the Metro de Medellín. A bus rapid-transit system called Transmetro, similar to Bogotá's TransMilenio, will begin operating in Barranquilla by late 2007. Cali's streets remain under construction as a new public-transit system called the Massive Integration of the West is being built.

Roads: The three main north-south highways are the Caribbean, Eastern, and Central Trunk Highways (*troncales*). Estimates of the length of Colombia's road system in 2004 ranged from

115,000 kilometers to 145,000 kilometers, of which fewer than 15 percent were paved. However, according to 2005 data reported by the Colombian government, the road network totaled 163,000 kilometers, 68 percent of which were paved and in good condition. The increase may reflect some newly built roads. President Uribe has vowed to pave more than 2,500 kilometers of roads during his administration, and about 5,000 kilometers of new secondary roads were being built in the 2003–6 period. Despite serious terrain obstacles, almost three-quarters of all cross-border dry cargo is now transported by road, 105,251 metric tons in 2005.

Railroads: Colombia has 3,034 kilometers of rail lines, 150 kilometers of which are 1.435-meter gauge and 3,154 kilometers, 0.914-meter gauge (2,611 kilometers of which are in use). Rail transport in Colombia remains underdeveloped. The national railroad system, once the country's main mode of transport for freight, has been neglected in favor of road development and now accounts for only about a quarter of freight transport. Passenger-rail use was suspended in 1992 and resumed at the end of the 1990s. However, fewer than 165,000 passenger journeys were made in 1999, as compared with more than 5 million in 1972, and the figure was only 160,130 in 2005. Short sections of railroad, mainly the Bogotá-Atlantic rim, are used to haul goods, mostly coal, to the Caribbean and Pacific ports. In 2005 a total of 27.5 million metric tons of cargo were transported by rail. Although the nation's rail network links seven of the country's 10 major cities, very little of it has been used regularly because of security concerns, lack of maintenance, and the power of the road transport union. During 2004–6, approximately 2,000 kilometers of the country's rail lines underwent refurbishment. This upgrade involved two main projects: the 1,484-kilometer line linking Bogotá to the Caribbean Coast and the 499-kilometer Pacific coastal network that links the industrial city of Cali and the surrounding coffee-growing region to the port of Buenaventura.

Ports: Seaports handle around 80 percent of international cargo. In 2005 a total of 105,251 metric tons of cargo were transported by water. Colombia's most important ocean terminals are Barranquilla, Cartagena, and Santa Marta on the Caribbean Coast and Buenaventura and Tumaco on the Pacific Coast. Exports mostly pass through the Caribbean ports of Cartagena and Santa Marta, while 65 percent of imports arrive at the port of Buenaventura. Other important ports and harbors are Bahía de Portete, Leticia, Puerto Bolívar, San Andrés, Santa Marta, and Turbo. Since privatization was implemented in 1993, the efficiency of port handling has increased greatly. There are plans to construct a deep-water port at Bahía Solano.

Inland Waterways: The main inland waterways total about 18,200 kilometers, 11,000 kilometers of which are navigable by riverboats. A well-developed and important form of transport for both cargo and passengers, inland waterways transport approximately 3.8 million metric tons of freight and more than 5.5 million passengers annually. Main inland waterways are the Magdalena–Cauca River system, which is navigable for 1,500 kilometers; the Atrato, which is navigable for 687 kilometers; the Orinoco system of more than five navigable rivers, which total more than 4,000 kilometers of potential navigation (mainly through Venezuela); and the Amazonas system, which has four main rivers totaling 3,000 navigable kilometers (mainly through Brazil). The government is planning an ambitious program to more fully utilize the main rivers for transport. In addition, the navy's riverine brigade has been patrolling waterways more aggressively in order to establish safer river transport in the more remote areas in the south and east of the country that are controlled by rebel groups.

Merchant Marine: The merchant marine totals 17 ships (1,000 gross registered tons or more), including four bulk, 13 cargo, one container, one liquefied gas, and three petroleum tanker ships. Colombia also has seven ships registered in other countries (Antigua and Barbuda, two; Panama, five).

Civil Aviation and Airports: Colombia has well-developed air routes and an estimated total of 984 airports, 100 of which have paved runways, plus two heliports. Of the 74 main airports, 20 can accommodate jet aircraft. Two airports are more than 3,047 meters in length, nine are 2,438–3,047 meters, 39 are 1,524–2,437 meters, 38 are 914–1,523 meters, 12 are shorter than 914 meters, and 880 have unpaved runways. The government has been selling its stake in local airports in order to allow their privatization. The country has 40 regional airports, and the cities of Bogotá, Medellín, Cali, Barranquilla, Bucaramanga, Cartagena, Cucutá, Letícia, Pereira, San Andrés, and Santa Marta have international airports. Bogotá's El Dorado International Airport handles 350 million metric tons of cargo and 8 million passengers a year, making it the largest airport in Latin America in terms of cargo and the third largest in passenger numbers.

Pipelines: Colombia has 4,350 kilometers of gas pipelines, 6,134 kilometers of oil pipelines, and 3,140 kilometers of refined-products pipelines. The country has five major oil pipelines, four of which connect with the Caribbean export terminal at Puerto Coveñas. Until at least September 2005, the United States funded efforts to help protect a major pipeline, the 769-kilometer-long Caño Limón–Puerto Coveñas pipeline, which carries about 20 percent of Colombia's oil production to Puerto Coveñas from the guerrilla-infested Arauca region in the eastern Andean foothills and Amazonian jungle. The number of attacks against pipelines began declining substantially in 2002. In 2004 there were only 17 attacks against the Caño Limón–Puerto Coveñas pipeline, down from 170 in 2001. However, a bombing in February 2005 shut the pipeline for several weeks, and attacks against the electrical gird system that provides energy to the Caño Limón oilfield have continued. New oil pipeline projects with Brazil and Venezuela are underway. In addition, the already strong cross-border trade links between Colombia and Venezuela were solidified in July 2004 with an agreement to build a US$320 million natural gas pipeline between the two countries, to be completed in 2008.

Telecommunications: Since being liberalized in 1991, the telecommunications sector has added new services, expanded coverage, improved efficiency, and lowered costs. The sector has had the second largest (after energy) investment in infrastructure (22 percent) since 1997. However, the economic downturn between 1999 and 2002 adversely affected telecommunications. During this period, Colombia's telecommunications industry lost US$2 billion despite a profit of US$1 billion in local service. In June 2003, the government liquidated the state-owned and heavily indebted National Telecommunications Company (Empresa Nacional de Telecomunicaciones—Telecom) and replaced it with Colombia Telecomunicaciones (Colombia Telecom). The measure enabled the industry to expand rapidly, and in 2004 it constituted 2.8 percent of gross domestic product (GDP). Telefónica of Spain acquired a 50 percent share in the company in 2006.

As a result of increasing competition, Colombia has a relatively modern telecommunications infrastructure that primarily serves larger towns and cities. Colombia's telecommunication system includes INTELSAT, 11 domestic satellite Earth stations, and a nationwide microwave radio relay system. The country's teledensity (the density of telephone lines in a community) is relatively high for Latin America (17 percent in 2006). However, there is a steep imbalance between rural and urban areas, with some regions below 10 percent and the big cities exceeding 30 percent. Bogotá, Medellín, and Cali account for about 50 percent of telephone lines in use. By the end of 2005, the number of telephone main lines in use totaled 7,851,649. Colombia Telecom accounted for only about 31 percent of these lines; 27 other operators accounted for the rest.

Colombia's mobile market is one of the fastest-growing businesses in the country. In mid-2004 mobile telephones overtook fixed lines in service for the first time. By 2005 Colombia had the highest mobile phone density (90 percent) in Latin America, as compared with the region's average density of 70 percent. The number of mobile telephone subscribers totaled an estimated 21.8 million in 2005, or 47.4 subscribers per 100 inhabitants, as compared with only 6.8 million in 2001.

Colombia is still far behind Brazil, Mexico, and Argentina in terms of online usage. It had an estimated total of 900,000 Internet subscribers by the end of 2005, a figure that equated to 4,739,000 Internet users, or 11.5 percent of the 2005 population (10.9 per 100 inhabitants). Colombia had 581,877 Internet hosts in 2006. Although as many as 70 percent of Colombians accessed the Internet over their ordinary telephone lines, dial-up access is losing ground to broadband. In 2005 Colombia had 345,000 broadband subscriber lines, or one per 100 inhabitants. In 2006 the number of personal computers per 1,000 people increased to an estimated 87 per 1,000 inhabitants, a rate still below that in other large Latin American economies.

In late 2004, Radio and Television of Colombia (Radio y Televisión de Colombia—RTVC) replaced the liquidated National Institute of Radio and Television (Instituto Nacional de Radio y Televisión—Inravisión) as the government-run radio and television broadcasting service, which oversees three national television stations and five radio companies (which operate about a dozen principal networks). Colombia has about 60 television stations, including seven low-power stations. In 2000 the population had about 11.9 million television receivers in use. Of the approximately 515 radio stations, 454 are AM; 34, FM; and 27, shortwave (see also Mass Media, below).

GOVERNMENT AND POLITICS

Government Overview: The Republic of Colombia is a constitutional, multiparty democracy under the constitution of July 1991. A unitary republic with a strong presidential regime, the national government has executive, legislative, and judicial branches established with separation of powers and with checks and balances. In the May 2006 presidential election, President Álvaro Uribe Vélez, a Liberal Party dissident, became the first president in 100 years to be reelected, thanks to a constitutional amendment authorizing re-election for consecutive terms. Moreover, he won by a record majority (62 percent, or 7.4 million votes) in the first round. With this strong electoral mandate and a working majority in Congress, President Uribe began his second term in August 2006. His congressional alliance includes independents and former Liberal Party members, as well as the Conservative Party (Partido Conservador—PC).

Although constitutional order and institutional stability have prevailed despite endemic violence stemming from guerrilla, paramilitary, and narcotics-trafficking activities, the violence and corruption associated with the enormous wealth created by the drug cartels have undermined the country's political and social foundations. Most Colombian government institutions have a reputation for inefficient, corrupt, and bureaucratic management. In particular, the military has been in the spotlight in recent years for corruption at high levels within the chain of command. Links between Colombia's various mini-trafficking organizations and its supposedly professional military continue to surface. Notable exceptions are reported to include the central bank, Ministry of Finance, and some other agencies responsible for economic policy formulation. With U.S. aid contingent on fighting corruption, the Uribe government reportedly has been making an effort to attack this pervasive problem. In 2005 perceptions of corruption improved slightly. However, Colombia ranked 59th of 163 countries in Transparency International's *Corruption Perceptions Index 2006* (it ranked 55th in the 2005 survey).

Executive Branch: As chief of state and head of government, the president has executive power and strong policy-making authority. Until 2005, the president was elected for a nonrenewable four-year term. That October the Constitutional Court endorsed the bill approved by Congress in December 2004 to incorporate presidential re-election into the 1991 constitution. Since May 2006, it has been possible for a president to be reelected for a second term. The constitution reestablished the position of vice president, who is elected on the same ticket as the president. By law, the vice president will succeed in the event of the president's resignation, illness, or death. The president heads and is assisted by a cabinet.

Legislative Branch: The bicameral Congress consists of a 102-member Senate (Senado) and a 166-member House of Representatives (Cámara de Representantes), which includes 161 members elected to represent the 32 departments and one to represent the Capital District, as well as an additional two members to represent the Afro-Colombian population, one member to represent the indigenous population, one to represent Colombians living abroad, and one for other political minorities. Members of both chambers are popularly elected for a four-year term with no re-election limit. Senators are elected by nationwide ballot; representatives are elected in multimember districts collocated within the 32 national departments. The Congress meets semiannually, and the president has the power to call it into special session, if required. Bogotá, as a separate federal district, elects its own representatives.

Judicial Branch: Colombia's judicial system is composed, at the highest level, of the coequal Supreme Court of Justice, Council of State, Constitutional Court, and Superior Judicial Council. The 23-member Supreme Court, which is divided into four chambers—civil cassation, criminal cassation, labor cassation, and constitutional procedure—rules on civil, criminal, and labor appeals and on constitutional procedure and administers various district superior, circuit, municipal, and lower courts. The 27-member Council of State supervises a system of administrative courts that scrutinize acts and decrees issued by executive and decentralized agencies. The nine-justice Constitutional Court is responsible for guarding the integrity and supremacy of the national constitution and reviewing the constitutionality of proposed legislation and international treaties before they are adopted officially. The 13-member Superior Judicial Council administers and disciplines the civilian justice system. Specialized circuit courts within the civil jurisdiction try cases involving particularly sensitive crimes such as narcotics trafficking and terrorism. The judicial system also includes the Office of the Attorney General (Fiscalía General de la Nación), which is an independent judicial agency headed by an independent attorney general (*fiscal*), who is elected for a four-year term by the Congress and is tasked with investigating criminal offenses and prosecuting the accused. At lower levels, the judicial system includes superior and municipal courts. Although the judicial branch is largely independent of the executive and legislative branches, Congress elects senior justices for eight-year terms on the basis of nominations made by judicial bodies or the president of the republic.

As part of the Ministry of Defense, the military justice system falls under the executive branch. The director of the military criminal justice system reports directly to the civilian minister of defense. The military justice system consists of the Supreme Military Tribunal, which serves as the court of appeals for all cases tried in military courts, and 40 military trial courts. The civilian Supreme Court serves as a second court of appeals for cases in which sentences of six or more years in prison are imposed. Although authorities rarely have brought to trial high-ranking officers of the security forces charged with human rights offenses, civilian courts tried a number of military personnel accused of human rights violations. The military judiciary may investigate and prosecute active-duty military and police personnel for crimes "related to acts of military service."

Administrative Divisions: The 1991 constitution converted Colombia's four intendancies (*intendencias*) and five commisaryships (*comisarías*) into administrative departments (*departamentos administrativos*), thereby increasing the number of departments to 32. They are: Amazonas, Antioquia, Araúca, Atlántico, Bolívar, Boyacá, Caldas, Caquetá, Casanaré, Cauca, César, Choco, Córdoba, Cundinamarca, Guainía, Guaviare, Huila, La Guajira, Magdalena, Meta, Nariño, Norte de Santander, Putumayo, Quíndio, Risaralda, San Andrés and Providencia, Santander, Sucre, Tolima, Valle del Cauca, Vaupés, and Vichada. These departments are divided into municipalities (*municipios*), each headed by a mayor (*alcalde*). Colombia had 1,061 municipalities in the 1993 census, but by 2005 that number had grown to 1,098. The charter also allows the creation of indigenous territories as self-governing territorial entities. The country's capital, Bogotá, is a separate capital district (Distrito Capital de Bogotá).

Provincial and Local Government: Under the 1991 constitution, citizens directly elect governors, deputies, mayors, municipal and district councils, and members of local administrative boards. Department governors are popularly elected for a four-year term and may not serve the subsequent term. Each department has a popularly elected Departmental Assembly (Asamblea Departamento) and a popularly elected corporation (Corporación) that oversees the actions of the governors. Each municipality has a popularly elected mayor and an administrative corporation, both of whom are elected for four-year terms and may not be reelected for the following term. The charter allows governors and mayors to hold popular consultations on issues within their purview. Departmental, district, and municipal comptrollers exercise, within their jurisdiction, functions similar to those of the comptroller general of the republic, that is, oversight of fiscal matters. As a separate capital district, Bogotá elects its own representatives, who may be reelected indefinitely. An important item on President Uribe's second-term agenda is to reduce the central government's very large deficit (more than 5 percent of gross domestic product) by limiting transfers of funds to regional governments, which accounted for 4.9 percent of gross domestic product in 2005.

Judicial and Legal System: The 1991 constitution strengthened the administration of justice by providing for the introduction of an oral, accusatory system to replace the traditional system, which was based on Spanish law and the Napoleonic Code, in order to expedite the judicial process and reduce the enormous backlog of cases. The transition to this U.S.-model system continues, and most of Colombia's major cities already have adopted it. The objective is for the whole system to be installed nationwide by 2008. The 1991 constitutional reforms also established the Office of the Attorney General (Fiscalía General de la Nación), which investigates and charges offenders. In addition, a people's defender (Defensor del Pueblo) oversees the Office of the Attorney General and ensures the protection of human rights. The legal system also includes an independent "control organ" called the Office of the Inspector General (Procuraduría), which directs the Public Ministry, an independent agency that investigates allegations of misconduct by public employees, including members of the state security forces. The people's defender is also under the Office of the Inspector General.

The government generally respects the rights, as provided by law, of freedom of speech, the press, assembly and association, religion, movement within the country, foreign travel, emigration, repatriation, granting of asylum or refugee status, and free and fair elections. In practice, the judicial system is overburdened, inefficient, and hindered by the suborning and intimidation of judges, prosecutors, and witnesses. Impunity remains a serious problem. The Supreme Court itself has acknowledged that perpetrators are punished in less than 1 percent of crimes. The civilian judiciary suffers from a backlog of cases to be processed, and these backlogs have led to large numbers of pretrial detainees.

Electoral System: Colombia has a democratically elected representative system with universal adult suffrage; the minimum voting age is 18. The National Electoral Council (Consejo Nacional Electoral—CNE) and the National Registrar's Office (Registraduría Nacional del Estado Civil) control the electoral process. The constitution allows citizens to directly elect, at the national level, the president and vice president of the republic as well as senators and representatives. If no candidate receives more than 50 percent of the vote in the first round, a runoff election between the two leading competitors is held about three weeks later. At the departmental and local levels, the constitution allows for citizens to directly elect governors, deputies, mayors, municipal and district council members, members of local administrative juntas, members of the Constituent Assembly, and other authorities and officials as the constitution may indicate. The most recent congressional elections were held in March 2002 and March 2006 and presidential elections, in May 2002 and May 2006. Legislative elections are next scheduled for March 2010 and the presidential election for May 2010. Regional elections for mayors and governors were held in October 2003, when independents were elected in the three largest cities, including Bogotá, and are scheduled for October 28, 2007.

Political Parties: Historically, Colombia maintained a two-party system in which two dominant but rival political parties alternated in power—the Liberals and the Conservatives, that is, the Liberal Party (Partido Liberal—PL) and the Conservative Party (Partido Conservador—PC). However, since the March 2002 congressional elections independent political forces have been gaining influence as the credibility of the two main parties has been tarnished by corruption and as distinctions between the two have been weakened. Thus, Colombia has become a multiparty system. In May 2002, Álvaro Uribe Veléz was elected the first independent president in

Colombian history. In the March 2006 congressional elections, the winners were the parties associated with President Uribe, which included the Conservative Party in an alliance with two "Uribista" groupings: Radical Change (Cambio Radical—CR) and Social Party of National Unity (Partido de la Unidad Nacional, or more commonly Partido de "la U"). Although the center-left Liberal Party is still the largest party in Congress, it remains a relatively powerless opposition party, along with the leftist Democratic Pole (Polo Democrático Alternativo—PDA). However, the Liberal Party has been moving to the center, while the PDA has been consolidating its ranks and expanding its grassroots support.

As a result of the March 2006 legislative elections, Colombia has 15 formally recognized political parties. In order to be recognized by the National Electoral Council (Consejo Nacional Electoral—CNE), a party must garner at least 2 percent of the vote in elections for the House of Representatives or the Senate. If a recognized party fails to gain at least 50,000 votes in a general election, it is dissolved automatically but may reincorporate at any time by presenting 50,000 signatures to the CNE. Political parties generally operate freely and without government interference. Members of independent parties may be elected to regional or local office and may also win seats in Congress. Dissidents from the two main parties also have chances to win elections.

Politics: Álvaro Uribe Vélez (president, 2002–6, 2006–), an independent, has proven to be a strong, capable, and exceptionally popular leader. He has consistently maintained popularity ratings of 70 to 80 percent, according to Gallup polls, since being elected in 2002, owing to his success in improving domestic security and socioeconomic conditions. In his first term in office, Uribe's accomplishments included containing the guerrillas, significantly reducing the high rates of criminal and political violence, and reviving economic growth. In order to address the need for a long-term national security strategy and to reinstate the rule of law and regain control over the country, the Uribe administration developed a "Democratic Security and Defense Policy," which is designed to combat the insurgency by providing internal security within a framework of democratic protections and guarantees. Uribe's hard-line strategy made him immensely popular, and he easily won re-election on May 28, 2006. In addition to focusing on security and military aspects of the security situation, the Uribe government has been spending time on international trade, supporting alternative means of development, and reforming the judicial and tax systems. Whether President Uribe achieves his second-term legislative priorities, including fiscal reforms and the ratification of the free-trade agreement with the United States, may depend on his ability to hold his congressional alliance together. This could prove difficult if the unity of the pro-Uribe (Uribista) coalition weakens during his second term. In a possible early indication of an apparent weakening political alliance in anticipation of the March 2010 elections, the Uribistas failed to gain control of the National Electoral Council in board elections in August 2006.

Mass Media: The law provides for freedom of speech and of the press, and the government generally has respected these rights in practice. Although security forces generally have not subjected journalists to harassment, intimidation, or violence, there have been exceptions, as well as reports of threats and violence against journalists by corrupt officials. Colombian journalists practice self-censorship to avoid reprisals by corrupt officials, criminals, and members of illegal armed groups. In the fifth annual *Reporters Without Borders Worldwide Press Freedom Index* published in October 2006, Colombia ranked 131 of a total of 168 countries, a decline from its

2005 ranking of 128. More than 80 journalists have been murdered in the past decade for doing their jobs.

Major international wire services, newspapers, and television networks have a presence in the country and generally operate free of government interference. Media ownership remains concentrated in the hands of wealthy families, large national conglomerates, or groups associated with one or the other of the two dominant political parties. The first foreign media owner in the country is the Spanish media conglomerate Prisa, which acquired majority ownership of the country's largest radio network. There are public television and radio networks and two news agencies (Ciep–El País and Colprensa).

Colombia has many national and regional television channels. The National Television Commission oversees television programming. Radio and Television of Colombia (Radio y Televisión de Colombia—RTVC), Colombia's principal television and radio operator, oversees three national television stations (two commercial and one educational) and five radio companies (which operate about a dozen principal networks). Television stations include Cadena Uno; Telecaribe; RCN TV, which is operated by Radio Cadena Nacional; and Caracol TV, a private commercial network. The country has two major national radio networks: Radiodifusora Nacional de Colombia, a state-run national radio; and Radio Cadena Nacional (RCN Radio), a medium-wave (AM) network with many affiliates. There are nine other principal networks, including Cadena Super, which includes Radio Super and Super Stereo FM; and Caracol, which runs several stations, including the flagship station Caracol Colombia. Many hundreds of radio stations are registered with the Ministry of Communications.

Several major newspapers and news magazines circulate nationally, and there are many influential regional publications. The press includes five main newspapers in Bogotá: *El Espacio*, an evening daily; *El Espectador*, a weekly; *El Nuevo Siglo*, a Conservative daily; *La República*, a business daily; and *El Tiempo*, a Liberal Party national daily. Other popular papers include Cali's *El País* and Medellín's *El Colombiano*, both Conservative dailies. Weekly news magazines published in Bogotá include *Cromos* and *Semana*.

Foreign Relations: Colombia has generally adopted a low profile, relying on international law and regional and international security organizations to pursue its interests. The country traditionally has had good relations with the United States, its most important foreign relationship. Although relations were strained during the presidency of Ernesto Samper (1994–98) because of his alleged drug connections, they have been excellent since the administration of Andrés Pastrana Arango (president, 1998–2002). In January 2000, the administration of President Bill Clinton pledged US$1.3 billion of mainly military assistance to Colombia to assist the antidrug component of Pastrana's six-year strategy to end the insurgency, eliminate drug trafficking, and promote economic and social development. In addition to increasing Colombia's counternarcotics capabilities by providing helicopters and training, this U.S. aid (known as Plan Colombia) was designed to support human rights, humanitarian assistance, alternative development, and economic and judicial reforms. Relations with the United States have been the foreign policy priority of President Uribe, who is an important ally in President George W. Bush's "war on terrorism" and "war on drugs." In addition to the challenge posed to the United States by Colombian drug trafficking, illegal Colombian immigrants in the United States are an issue in U.S.-Colombian relations. In early 2003, Colombia ranked among the world's top seven exporters of illegal aliens to the United States.

Regional relations remain good despite occasional issues with neighbors, especially regarding spillover from Colombia's civil conflict, including cross-border guerrilla crossings, the flow of refugees, and the spread of drug crops. These issues are of particular concern to the bordering countries of Brazil, Ecuador, Panama, Peru, and Venezuela. For example, although cooperation between Colombia and Ecuador on border security issues has increased in recent years, Colombia's U.S.-financed aerial drug-eradication program created new tensions in bilateral relations over Ecuador's complaint that sprayed chemicals were drifting over the border and destroying agriculture on the Ecuadorian side. In response, Colombia suspended spraying along the border in January 2006. However, a new row erupted in December 2006 over Colombia's renewed spraying. Peru has been concerned over incursions of Revolutionary Armed Forces of Colombia (Fuerzas Armadas Revolucionarias de Colombia—FARC) units into Peruvian territory, reports that the FARC has made contact with the Shining Path rebels in Peru, and satellite images showing that there are drug cultivations springing up along the Colombia–Peru border.

Brazil, which is now the second-largest market in the world for Colombian cocaine after the United States, is known to be a major outlet for Colombian cocaine and a source for weapons for Colombian guerrilla and paramilitary groups. The Brazilian government of President Luiz Inácio Lula da Silva, in contrast to its predecessors, cooperated with Colombian security forces in joint antiguerrilla operations along the Brazil–Colombia border in an attempt to control this cross-border trafficking. Brazil is also concerned about FARC drug links with the ultraviolent Brazilian prison gang called the First Command of the Capital.

Panama also has been affected by cross-border terrorism and other activities by Colombian armed groups, such as a raid by paramilitary forces against Panamanian border settlements and the resulting killings of several leaders of indigenous communities in early 2003. In addition, Panama has had to forcibly repatriate Colombian refugees. In an attempt to improve border security, Colombia and Panama signed a bilateral agreement in April 2003.

Relations with Nicaragua and Venezuela have been strained over territorial disputes. The International Court of Justice at The Hague continues to review Nicaragua's claim of sovereignty rights over the Colombian islands of San Andrés y Providencia and the archipelago's surrounding Caribbean waters. In July 2002, the dispute flared up when Nicaragua began offering offshore oil concessions near the disputed waters. The Colombian navy began increasing its patrolling activity around San Andrés. Bilateral committees also are negotiating with Venezuela over waters in the Gulf of Venezuela. Other issues with Venezuela include the ambivalent stance of the Venezuelan president, Hugo Chávez Frías, toward the Colombian guerrillas, who have long had camps on the Venezuelan side of the border and use Venezuela as a logistics base; the presence of undocumented Colombians in Venezuela; and activities in Venezuela of Colombian narcotics traffickers.

Under the Uribe administration, Colombia's relations with the European Union (EU) have been cool, and the EU has been critical of President Uribe's hard-line, United States–supported counterinsurgency strategy. The EU is particularly concerned that President Uribe's approach, such as granting amnesty to right-wing paramilitaries, increases the potential for human rights abuses within Colombia. In 2004 the EU withheld its support of the Uribe government's peace initiative with paramilitaries for lack of a credible and comprehensive peace strategy, and EU aid to Colombia has been limited to social investment. Since José Luis Rodríguez Zapatero became prime minister in March 2004, Spain's diplomatic stance toward Colombia also has been cool.

Membership in International Organizations: The major organizations in which Colombia is a member include: the Agency for the Prohibition of Nuclear Weapons in Latin America and the Caribbean, Andean Pact, Caribbean Development Bank, Economic Commission for Latin America and the Caribbean, Food and Agriculture Organization of the United Nations, Group of 3, Group of 11, Group of 24, Group of 77, Inter-American Development Bank, International Atomic Energy Agency, International Bank for Reconstruction and Development, International Chamber of Commerce, International Civil Aviation Organization, International Confederation of Free Trade Unions, International Criminal Police Organization (Interpol), International Development Association, International Finance Corporation, International Fund for Agricultural Development, International Labor Organisation, International Maritime Organization, International Maritime Satellite Organization, International Monetary Fund, International Olympic Committee, International Organization for Migration, International Organization for Standardization, International Telecommunication Union, International Telecommunications Satellite Organization, Latin American Economic System, Latin American Integration Association, Non-Aligned Movement, Organization of American States, Permanent Court of Arbitration, Rio Group, United Nations, United Nations Conference on Trade and Development, United Nations Educational, Scientific and Cultural Organization, United Nations Industrial Development Organization, United Nations Office of the High Commissioner for Refugees, Universal Postal Union, World Confederation of Labor, World Federation Of Trade Unions, World Health Organization, World Intellectual Property Organization, World Meteorological Organization, World Tourism Organization, and World Trade Organization.

Major International Agreements and Treaties: Defense treaties to which Colombia is a party include the Inter-American Treaty of Reciprocal Assistance of 1947 (the Rio Treaty). Regional treaties include the Andean Pact, now known as the Andean Community, which also includes Bolivia, Ecuador, Peru, and Venezuela and the bodies and institutions making up the Andean Integration System (AIS). Colombia has also signed, adhered to, and ratified 105 international treaties or agreements relating to the environment. These include the Antarctic Treaty, Biodiversity, Climate Change, Desertification, Endangered Species, Hazardous Wastes, Marine Life Conservation, Nuclear Test Ban, Ozone Layer Protection, Ship Pollution, Tropical Timber 83, Tropical Timber 94, and Wetlands conventions or agreements. Colombia has signed, but not ratified, the Antarctic-Environmental Protocol, Law of the Sea, and Marine Dumping. Colombia is a signatory of the Treaty on the Non-Proliferation of Nuclear Weapons and is also a party to the Treaty for the Prohibition of Nuclear Weapons in Latin America (the Tlatelolco Treaty). By 1975 signatories to the 1974 Declaration of Ayacucho, including Colombia, had decided on limitations to nuclear, biological, and chemical weapons.

NATIONAL SECURITY

Armed Forces Overview: Under the constitution, the president is commander in chief of the Armed Forces of Colombia (Fuerzas Armadas de Colombia—FAC), which consists of the army (Ejército Nacional); navy (Armada Nacional), including naval aviation, marines, and coast guard; air force (Fuerza Aérea Colombiana); and paramilitary National Police (Policía Nacional—PN). The civilian-led Ministry of National Defense is responsible for internal and external security and oversees the armed forces. It also has organizational control over the National Police. In practice, however, the president exercises direct command over the military and the police, leaving the minister of defense with only administrative duties. The commanders of the three services (army, navy, and air force) are responsible to the commander general of the armed forces, who reports directly to the Ministry of Defense. The Superior Council of Defense and Security (Consejo Superior de Defensa y Seguridad—CSDS) and the Security Council advise the president. The FAC is responsible for maintaining order and security in rural areas and supports the PN in urban areas when called upon. In 2005 the active armed forces totaled 209,000, including 74,700 conscripts. The armed forces strength by service was as follows: army 180,000, including 63,800 conscripts; navy 22,000, including 100 naval aviation, 14,000 marines, and 7,000 conscripts; and air force 7,000, including some 3,900 conscripts. Reservists totaled an additional 238,700 (army, 232,700; navy, 4,800; and air force, 1,200).

Foreign Military Relations: Since the late 1980s, the United States has been the primary provider of military training and equipment to Colombia. Other important suppliers have included Brazil, Spain, France, Germany, Italy, and Israel. Many Colombian military personnel have received training in the United States or U.S. training in Colombia; the United States has provided equipment to the Colombian military and police through the military assistance program, foreign military sales program, and international narcotics control program. In 1999–2001 the U.S. government approved a US$1.3 billion aid package called Plan Colombia, most of which was earmarked for military hardware for antidrug efforts, such as a fleet of 71 helicopters for spraying coca fields. In March 2002, in response to a request from President George W. Bush, the U.S. Congress lifted restrictions on U.S. assistance to Colombia to allow it to be used for counterinsurgency in addition to antidrug operations. U.S. support for Colombia's counternarcotics efforts included slightly more than US$2.5 billion in aid between 2000 and 2004, making Colombia the third-largest recipient of U.S. aid, after Israel and Egypt. Although Plan Colombia ended in 2005, the United States has continued funding it with aid for counterinsurgency and counternarcotics efforts averaging US$600 million per year through 2007.

U.S. military aid is devoted primarily to training units of the Special Forces and Rapid Deployment Force. The "cap" on U.S. troops and contractors in Colombia was raised in October 2004 from about 320 U.S. military trainers and 400 U.S. civilian contractors to 800 military personnel and 600 civilian contractors. These U.S. personnel help the Colombian armed forces to develop commando squads dedicated to capturing or killing rebel commanders. With U.S. assistance, President Uribe has been attempting to make the armed forces more professional, to build a countrywide civilian informant network, and to try to involve the civilian population in his Democratic Security and Defense Policy.

External Threat: Colombia does not face any known foreign threats. Venezuela is the only neighbor that might pose a potential military challenge over as-yet unresolved territorial disputes relating to the maritime boundary, where there may be oilfields. The largely state-controlled Venezuelan media portray Colombia as an external aggressor with U.S. backing. However, since the two nations concluded a bilateral free-trade agreement in 1991, Colombia and Venezuela have not allowed the occasional security incidents involving Colombian guerrillas and paramilitaries along their long common border to escalate into a serious issue.

Defense Budget: As a result of U.S. aid under Plan Colombia, the defense budget, as a share of gross domestic product (GDP), expanded during the 2000–6 period from 3.2 percent of GDP in 2000 to 6 percent of GDP in 2006. In dollar terms, estimates for the defense budget for 2006 ranged from US$4.1 billion to nearly US$4.5 billion. President Uribe's defense budget increases have gone toward expanding the armed forces, mainly the number of professional soldiers and counterguerrilla battalions.

Major Military Units: The army is organized into six divisions consisting of 17 brigades (six mechanized, two air-portable, and nine infantry), the Army Aviation Brigade, the Antinarcotics Brigade, the Special Forces Brigade, the Training Brigade, and two artillery battalions. The infantry includes 47 infantry battalions—four air-transportable, three antinarcotics, one ceremonial, 22 counterinsurgency, five high-mountain, four jungle, three mechanized, four military police, and one special forces. Armor consists of nine cavalry groups, including one air-transportable; artillery, nine battalions, including one air defense; engineers, 10 battalions; and logistics, 15 battalions. The navy is organized into four fleet commands (including five marine battalions), a coast guard, and a naval air arm. The 14,000-member Colombian Marine Corps is organized into a single division with two brigades (one amphibious assault brigade and one riverine brigade), each with two battalions. The air force is organized into four functional commands: combat, transport, training, and logistical support. The Combat Air Command includes six combat groups—two fighter squadrons, a tactical air support command, a utility/armed helicopter command, a military air transport command, and an air training command.

Major Military Equipment: The army inventory includes 12 light tanks, 182 reconnaissance vehicles, about 200 armored personnel carriers, 20 antitank guided weapons, and about 100 helicopters. The navy has four submarines, eight principal surface combatants, 27 patrol and coastal combatants, five offshore patrol vessels, nine coastal/inshore patrol vessels, and 13 riverine patrol boats. The navy inventory also includes at least three Orca-class fast intercept craft and three sail training ships. The air force inventory includes 57 combat aircraft and 23 armed helicopters. In 2006 the air force signed for 25 Brazilian Embraer EMB–314 Super Tucano light attack aircraft and took delivery of the first five in December. The air force's fleet of Israel Aerospace Industries Kfir C2s and C7s and Dassault Aviation Mirage 5 COAs and CODs, which have been in service more than 30 years, need to be upgraded or replaced. The paramilitary National Police force has 28 aircraft and 10 helicopters.

Military Service: Under the 1991 constitution, all nonstudent males reaching the age of 18 must present themselves for military service of one to two years (normally 24 months). However, those from well-off families can buy their way out of serving, and those with high-school diplomas are exempt from combat. In effect, mostly the poor with little education actually serve. After completing active service, conscripts become part of the reserves. In 2005 an estimated 389,735 males aged 18 to 49 reached military service age. In this age-group, a total of 10,212,456 males were available for military service, and an estimated 6,986,228 were deemed fit for military service. As of 1993, females may volunteer for military service, which could be required if warranted by circumstances. In 2005 an estimated 383,146 females aged 18 to 49 reached military service age. In this age--group, 10,561,562 females were available for military service, and an estimated 8,794,465 were deemed fit for military service.

Military Forces Abroad: Colombia has one infantry battalion in Egypt in support of the Multinational Force and Observers (MFO), an independent international peacekeeping organization established by Egypt and Israel to monitor the security arrangements of their 1979 Treaty of Peace. The paramilitary National Police deployed personnel to serve with United Nations peacekeeping forces in Croatia and El Salvador.

Security Forces: In 2005 the security forces totaled 129,000 personnel, including 121,000 members of the paramilitary National Police (Policía Nacional—PN) and 8,000 members of the rural militia. Although the PN and the military forces are formally independent institutions, with their own budgets and personnel, the PN is organizationally subordinate to the Ministry of Defense. In addition to supporting the army in its internal security role, the PN shares law enforcement duties, with the exception of investigative functions, with the Administrative Department of Security (Departamento Administrativo de Seguridad—DAS) and the Attorney General's Technical Investigation Corps (Cuerpo Técnico de Investigación—CTI). The highly trained Groups of Unified Action for Personal Freedom (Grupos de Acción Unificada por la Libertad Personal—Gaula) have long enjoyed U.S. support and have a fleet of Blackhawk helicopters and aircraft for the tasks of drug crop eradication and antikidnapping and urban hostage-rescue operations. One of Colombia's most effective counternarcotics forces, the 200-member Directorate of the Judicial Police and Investigation (Dirección de Policía Judicial e Investigación—DIJIN) is a U.S.-trained and -funded force. Under the January 2007 reorganization of the National Police, the DIJIN was renamed the Criminal Investigation Directorate (Dirección de Investigación Criminal—DIC).

Internal Threat: Colombia's principal internal threats are posed by illegal armed organizations, mainly the Revolutionary Armed Forces of Colombia (Fuerzas Armadas Revolucionarias de Colombia—FARC), but also paramilitary groups and narcotics-trafficking syndicates. These organizations cannot be neatly separated because the insurgent and paramilitary groups are heavily involved in the illegal narcotics trade, and the narcotics traffickers have been known to use the guns-for-hire services of the paramilitaries. Although the country's largest paramilitary organization, the United Self-Defense Forces of Colombia (Autodefensas Unidas de Colombia— AUC), was formally demobilized in 2006, basically on its own terms, critics complained that many of the demobilized "paramilitaries" proved to be common criminals taking advantage of the lenient amnesty to clean their records. Even after having won immunity from prosecution from previous crimes, many reportedly have continued their illegal operations by simply being recycled into new paramilitary groups or signing up to staff the armed wings of the drug traffickers. In August 2006, an estimated 2,000 paramilitaries belonged to other groups that have remained outside the peace process altogether.

The main guerrilla organizations that continue to be active are the FARC, the National Liberation Army (Ejército de Liberación Nacional—ELN), and the much smaller People's Liberation Army (Ejército de Liberación Popular—EPL). The FARC is the best-equipped, -trained, and -organized guerrilla force in Latin America and poses the primary insurgency threat to the Colombian government. It has an estimated 16,000 active rural combatants and between 4,000 and 5,000 urban militants. The ELN, with an estimated 3,200 members plus an urban militia of undetermined size, continues to be a significant threat, specializing in economic sabotage, particularly of the oil industry but also the transportation and communications infrastructure. The EPL has an estimated 300 members.

The Uribe government has rejected guerrilla demands for prisoner exchanges and demilitarized zones as a precondition for peace talks. After repeated efforts to initiate a peace process with the FARC failed, the Uribe government, with the support of the United States under Plan Colombia, sought a more confrontational approach through a sustained military offensive against the FARC in its rural strongholds. It is generally believed that the left-wing guerrillas have little chance of taking power in Colombia. Nevertheless, the FARC and ELN remain well funded and well equipped and are capable of carrying out effective guerrilla attacks against the military and security forces, as well as occasional acts of urban terrorism in Bogotá. The FARC's failure to disrupt the presidential election of May 2006 demonstrated that it lacks the military capacity to destabilize much less overthrow the government. Nevertheless, the continuing stalemate also has shown that the government lacks the ability to defeat the FARC through military means.

In contrast with the FARC, the more politically inclined ELN has agreed to meet government representatives, such as in Havana, Cuba, in December 2005, to discuss the possibility of a peace process. As a result, more serious negotiations between the ELN and the Uribe government were expected to be held during President Uribe's second term. On October 26, 2006, after several rounds of exploratory talks in Havana, the Colombian government and the ELN announced the start of formal peace negotiations to take place in November and December 2006.

According to Colombian government figures, at least 2,387 guerrillas (1,558 FARC members and 359 ELN members) and 470 AUC members deserted their respective organizations in 2006 under Colombia's program to rehabilitate former combatants. The deserters included 384 minors and 425 women. As of the end of 2006, 11,264 irregulars had laid down their arms on an individual basis since President Uribe took office in August 2002.

In addition to the aforementioned insurgent and paramilitary threats, violent crime by common criminals is rampant in Colombia's major cities and often carried out with impunity. Homicide levels are among the highest in the world, fueled by high unemployment, growing poverty, the ready availability of guns, and the growth of drug trafficking and organized crime. Unlike the guerrilla groups, the narcotics traffickers are more active in urban areas, spawning many homicides among competing groups. Criminal bands specializing in kidnapping, extortion, and robbery target businesses and civilians. Kidnapping exceeded a record 3,700 reported cases in 2000; guerrilla and paramilitary groups were responsible for about three-quarters of them. According to the Ministry of Defense, in 2006 the number of kidnapping cases totaled 249, compared with 376 in 2005. In addition to improved law enforcement, the decline resulted from the government's offensive against the guerrillas and the demobilization of many paramilitaries.

Approximately the same number of kidnappings (800) were reported in 2005. Guerrilla and paramilitary groups may still be responsible for more than two-thirds of kidnappings; organized crime, for about one-third. The most vulnerable targets are campesinos and local businessmen. The insurgency has left much of the Colombian countryside planted with guerrilla landmines, which killed 1,100 people in the year ending in June 2006, the highest landmine casualty rate in the world. Although most of the casualties are soldiers, 30 percent are civilians, almost all of them campesinos.

After drug trafficking, the main illicit industries are contraband, forgery (principally of clothing, books, CDs, and audio- and video-cassettes), and, more recently, theft of gasoline. Contraband is a major industry. A significant amount of foreign exchange is believed to be from illegal trade in gold and emeralds, in addition to drugs. In 1999 the value of contraband in Colombia increased to US$2.2 billion, more than doubling in a decade. The amount accounted for about 25 percent of total imports and 50 percent of total exports. According to a study by the U.S. Treasury Department, Colombia and North Korea are the largest producers of counterfeit U.S. banknotes, and Colombia is also the number-one source of counterfeit money in the United States, accounting for about 15 percent of the 56.2 million counterfeit dollars in circulation in 2005.

Narcotics Production and Trafficking: Other than kidnapping and extortion, the principal activities of organized crime and the armed groups in Colombia are narcotics production and trafficking, mainly of cocaine and heroin, and these activities also have involved the guerrilla and paramilitary forces. Trafficking in processed cocaine and other illicit drugs accounts for more than US$5 billion a year and represents between 2.0 percent and 2.5 percent of gross domestic product a year. Only an estimated half of these illicit revenues return to Colombia. The Revolutionary Armed Forces of Colombia (Fuerzas Armadas Revolucionarias de Colombia—FARC) and the National Liberation Army (Ejército de Liberación Nacional—ELN) control all aspects of the drug trade in their areas of influence. For example, they levy taxes at all levels of the narcotics production chain. Since 2004 many Colombian drug traffickers have been joining or buying their way into the paramilitary militias in order to qualify for an immunity program.

Latin America's largest exporter of illegal drugs, Colombia is the world's leading coca cultivator and supplier of refined cocaine. More than 90 percent of the cocaine that enters the United States is produced, processed, or transshipped in Colombia. The country is also a growing source for heroin. Although opium poppy cultivation fell 50 percent to 2,100 hectares between 2003 and 2004, it yielded a potential 3.8 metric tons of pure heroin, mostly for the U.S. market. Despite tactical successes (such as the dismantling of the big cartels in the 1980s), large amounts of U.S. military and financial support for the government's war on drugs, and an active aerial eradication program, coca cultivation more than doubled between 1995 and 1999. Increased aerial spraying under Plan Colombia reduced the coca-growing area under cultivation by one-half between 2001 and 2004, but aggressive replanting allowed this area to expand in 2005. As much coca reportedly was being cultivated in Colombia in 2006 as when aerial spraying of the drug crop began in 2000. Coca cultivating simply has been redistributed into smaller, harder-to-reach crops. For these reasons, an investigative report published in the *New York Times* in August 2006 described the US$4.7 billion Plan Colombia as a failure, pointing out that, despite counternarcotics efforts since the mid-1980s, the supply of cocaine on U.S. streets has remained virtually unchanged, prices have fallen, and purity has increased.

Human Rights: The constitution provides for freedom of speech and the press, and the government generally respects these rights in practice. Individuals criticize the government both publicly and in private. The media express a wide spectrum of political viewpoints and often sharply criticize the government, all without fear of government reprisal. However, Colombia is one of the world's most dangerous countries in which to practice the profession of journalism; a number of journalists are killed almost every year, and journalists continue to work in an atmosphere of threats and intimidation, in some instances from corrupt local officials in collaboration with paramilitary groups, but primarily from terrorist groups. Journalists practice self-censorship to avoid retaliation and harassment by criminals and members of illegal armed groups.

According to the U.S. Department of State's 2006 human rights report, the government's respect for human rights continued to improve, despite the persistence of serious problems. Civilian authorities generally maintained effective control of the military and security forces, but there were instances in which elements of the security forces acted in violation of state policy. President Uribe generally has been quick to hold senior military officials accountable for criminal incidents within the ranks, causing considerable turnover in the military high command. Amnesty International charged in September 2006 that there had been no substantive improvement in the human rights situation, that human rights conditions had worsened in several conflict zones, and that collusion between the armed forces and illegal paramilitary groups was continuing. The government has taken steps to improve the human rights situation. Government statistics noted that, in 2005, killings decreased by 10 percent, terrorist massacres by nearly 4 percent, killings of trade union leaders by 67 percent, and forced displacements by more than 27 percent. According to authorities, the number of homicides during 2005 was the lowest in 18 years.

The National Penitentiary Institute (Instituto Nacional Penitenciario y Carcelario—INPEC) manages the country's 139 national prisons and is responsible for inspecting municipal jails. Many of INPEC's 8,757 prison guards in 2005 were poorly trained or corrupt. Police, prison guards, and military forces routinely mistreat detainees. Conditions in the severely overcrowded and underfunded prisons are harsh, especially for prisoners without significant outside support, and prisoners frequently rely on bribes for favorable treatment. The government does not hold political prisoners, although in 2005 it held 4,721 prisoners accused of terrorism, rebellion, or aiding and abetting insurgency.